AF594407

BULLDOZERS

Paul Zachary

CONSTRUCTION MACHINES

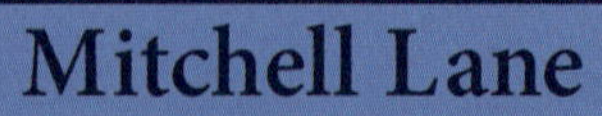

PUBLISHERS

2001 SW 31st Avenue
Hallandale, FL 33009
www.mitchelllane.com

First Edition, 2021.

Author: Paul Zachary
Designer: Ed Morgan
Editor: Morgan Brody

Little Mitchie is an imprint of Mitchell Lane Publishers.

Title: Construction Machines: Bulldozers / by Paul Zachary
Description: Hallandale, FL :
Mitchell Lane Publishers, [2021]

Series: Construction Machines
Library bound ISBN: 978-1-68020-684-5
eBook ISBN: 978-1-68020-685-2

Photo credits: Shutterstock, freepik.com

CONTENTS

Words in **bold** can be found in the Glossary.

Push! Push! Push!
The bulldozer clears the land.

tracks

The bulldozer runs on **tracks** instead of wheels. The tracks go over rocks, mud, dirt, and **debris**. It doesn't get stuck.

tractor
cab

The tractor is the body of the bulldozer. It includes the **cab** where the controls are located. The **operator** sits in the cab.

Safety First! The operator should wear a hard hat, goggles, gloves, and a safety vest.

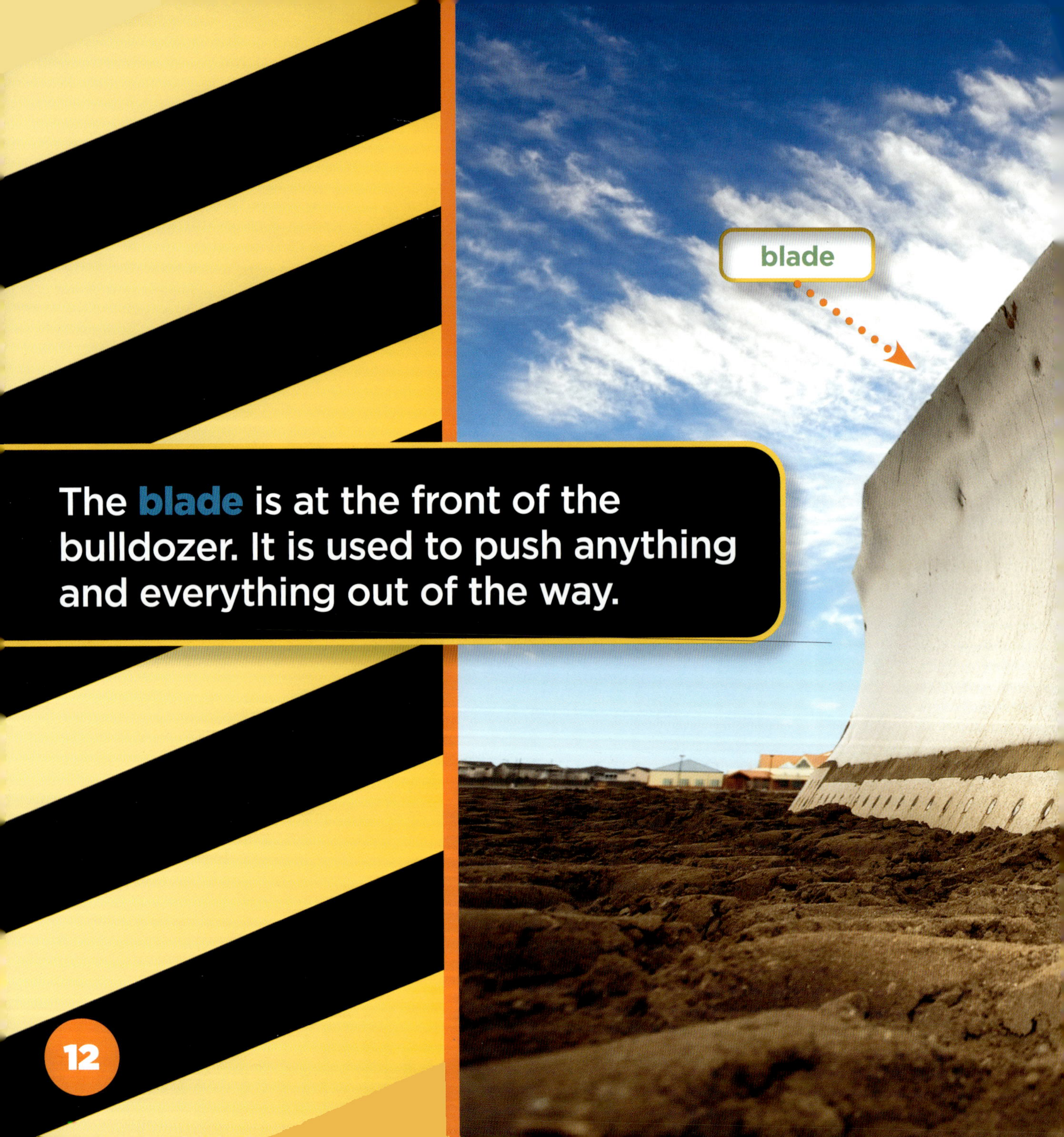

The **blade** is at the front of the bulldozer. It is used to push anything and everything out of the way.

The ripper is at the back of some bulldozers. It rips up anything and everything on the ground.

ripper

Bulldozers have big **diesel engines** since they move heavy materials. Diesel engines are very loud.

diesel engine

Bulldozers are also used to push trees over. They are helpful at landfills to move trash around. They can even be used to clear snow off roads.

Bulldozers do important work. It's hard to imagine a **construction** site without these heavy machines.

INTERESTING FACTS

- There are three types of bulldozers to choose from depending on the specific project.
    - Crawler Bulldozer or the track bulldozer looks like a tractor. It is great for moving heavy materials from one area to another. Larger crawlers have rippers to crush and clear **terrain**.
    - Wheel Bulldozer or the tire bulldozer is larger than the crawler. It is easier to maneuver and is ideal for soft or sensitive ground.
    - Mini Bulldozer or the compact bulldozer is great for projects that require more versatility than the larger machinery.
- The average bulldozer can go about 6 mph which is the same speed as a bicycle.
- A bulldozer can go faster backward than forward.
- The average bulldozer weighs over 300,000 lbs.

GLOSSARY

blade
The flat, sharp-edged part of a tool

cab
The part of a tractor where the driver sits

construction
The process of building something, such as a house or a street

debris
Rubble, trash, garbage

diesel engines
Engines that burn diesel fuel and are often used in heavy machines

operator
The person who works a machine

terrain
A piece of land

tracks
A metal band that wraps around the wheels of a bulldozer

SOURCES

Reinke, Beth Bence. *Bulldozers* Push!, 2017.

Blippi. *Construction Trucks with Blippi*. 2017.

FURTHER READING

Bell, Samantha. *Bulldozer*. North Mankato, MN: Cherry Lake Publishers, 2019

Murray, Julie. *Bulldozers*. North Mankato, MN: Abdo Publishing Company, 2019

INDEX

ABOUT THE AUTHOR

PAUL ZACHARY has recently moved into a new community. He is fascinated by all the construction machines used to build streets, sidewalks, new homes, and even tennis courts. Watching the bulldozer at work was particularly exciting as he watched new homes being built.